Pulleys

by Michael Dahl

Bridgestone Books
an Imprint of Capstone Press

Bridgestone Books are published by Capstone Press
818 North Willow Street, Mankato, Minnesota 56001
Copyright © 1996 by Capstone Press
Printed in the United States of America

Library of Congress Cataloging-in-Publication Data
Dahl, Michael S.
    Pulleys/by Michael S. Dahl
    p. cm. -- (Early reader science. Simple machines)
    Includes bibliographical references and index.
    Summary: Describes many different kinds, uses, and benefits of pulleys.
    ISBN 1-56065-445-7
    1. Pulleys--Juvenile literature. [1. Pulleys.] I. Title. II. Series
TJ147.D324 1996
621.8'11--dc20

                                                96-27769
                                                CIP
                                                 AC

Photo credits
FPG/Dennis Cox, 8. International Stock/Michael Phillip Manheim, 14.
Unicorn/Eric R. Berndt, 4, 12; Andre Jenny, 16; Aneal Vohra, 10; cover.
Visuals Unlimited/A. Copley, 6; John D. Cunningham, 18.

Table of Contents

Words in **boldface** type in the text are defined in the Words to Know section in the back of this book.

Machines

Machines are any **tools** that help people do work. A pulley is a machine. Pulleys help us lift **loads**.

What Is a Pulley?

A pulley is a small wheel. Pulleys work with ropes and chains. The rope or chain fits into a **groove** on the pulley. The groove keeps the rope or chain from slipping off.

Pulley Systems

When pulleys and ropes or chains work together, they are called a pulley system. Pulleys can be large or small. They can be made of metal, wood, or plastic. Pulleys with two wheels side by side are called blocks.

Single Fixed Pulley

A single fixed pulley has one wheel that stays in place. Single fixed pulleys do not give people more power. They only help people move things up or down. Flagpoles have single fixed pulleys for raising and lowering flags.

Single Movable Pulley

A pulley tied to the load itself is called a single movable pulley. The single movable pulley gives people more power. With a single movable pulley, people can lift twice as much weight as they can without one.

Pulleys in Action

A ski lift uses single movable pulleys. Ski lift chairs have pulleys on top. A **cable** lifts the chairs off the ground and up the snowy hill. The ski lift also brings the chairs back down.

More than One Wheel

More wheels give a pulley system more strength. A drawbridge uses a pulley system with several pulleys and cables working together. A heavy drawbridge opens easily because of its pulley system.

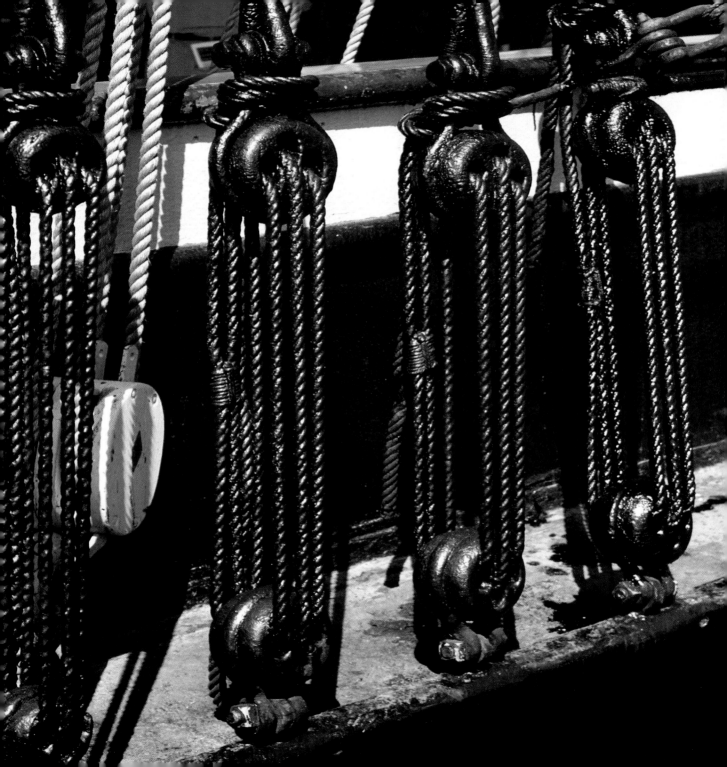

Block and Tackle

A block and tackle is a kind of pulley system that uses one rope with many different wheels. A block and tackle gives us more **force** for moving objects. Sailors use a block and tackle for lifting heavy sails on their ships. Circus workers use a block and tackle to lift their giant tents.

Cranes

Cranes are huge machines that lift heavy loads high into the air. Most cranes get their strength from pulley systems. Buildings and bridges could not be built without the power of pulleys.

Hands On: Make Your Own Block and Tackle Pulley System

What You Need

- Two brooms or broom handles
- A long rope
- Two friends

What You Do

1. Have your friends face each other, standing about six feet (about two meters) apart.
2. Each friend should hold a broom handle. They should hold the broom handles chest high in front of them with both hands.
3. Tie the rope to one broom handle.
4. Wrap the rope back and forth around both handles. Wrap it at least four or five times. This is your block and tackle.
5. Hold onto the end of the rope and stand about six feet (about two meters) behind one of your friends.
6. Tell your friends to keep the broom handles from getting closer to each other.
7. Pull on your end of the rope.

Your friends cannot stand still. They will be pulled toward each other. The block and tackle you made gives you greater strength. Try out this trick with two adults and you should still be stronger than they are.

Words to Know

cable—strong, heavy rope, often made of metal

force—physical power, strength

groove—a smooth pathway carved into the surface of a tool

load—anything force is applied upon

tool—anything a person uses to get a job done

Read More

Ardley, Neil. *The Science Book of Machines.* New York: Harcourt Brace Jovanovich, 1992.

James, Elizabeth. *The Simple Facts of Simple Machines.* New York: Lothrop, Lee & Shepard, 1975.

Rowe, Julian and Molly Perham. *Make It Move!* Chicago: Children's Press, 1993.

Stephen, R. J. *Cranes.* New York: Franklin Watts, 1986.

Index